BARRY

The Official Kerryman Joke Book

By Des MacHale

THE MERCIER PRESS

The Mercier Press
P.O. Box 5, 5 French Church St., Cork.
24 Lower Abbey Street, Dublin 1.

ISBN 0 85342 609 0

(Reprinted 1981)
(Reprinted 1982)
(Reprinted 1983)
(Reprinted 1984)
(Reprinted 1986)
(Reprinted 1988)
(Reprinted 1990)
(Reprinted 1992)

Nihil Obstat: Daniel O'Connell
Imprimatur: + Cardinal Rinucinni.

Printed in Ireland by Litho Press Co., Midleton, Co. Cork.

INTRODUCTION

Here it is at last folks – *The Official Kerryman Jokebook.* Admittedly there have been two unofficial books entitled – *The Book of Kerryman Jokes* and *The Worst Kerryman Jokes,* but this book is the real thing, complete with Imprimatur.

Despite the predictions of the prophets of doom, the popularity of the Kerryman joke has never decreased. It is a creative joke form peculiar to Ireland and there is very little truth in the frequently heard assertion that Kerryman jokes are merely rehashed versions of the anti-Irish jokes so common in England. In fact, the previous books of Kerryman jokes have sold so well and enjoyed such a wide circulation, that many of the recent anti-Irish jokes that have surfaced are direct adapations of Kerryman jokes, which are guaranteed Irish.

Kerrymen of course can and do take all the jokes in the spirit in which they are offered. Since Kerry's annihilation of Dublin and the 1978 football final, Kerrymen are riding on the crest of a wave, and it would take more than jokes to ruffle them. I am pleased to report that I have never received a single angry letter or rebuke from a Kerryman, and that is only how it should be.

A Kerryman went to confession and when he had confessed his sins he was told by the priest to say the Our Father for his penance.
'I'm afraid I don't know that prayer,' said the Kerryman.
'How about the Hail Mary?' said the priest.
'I don't know that either,' said the Kerryman.
'Is there any prayer you do know?' asked the priest.
'Yes,' said the Kerryman, 'there's the Angelus.'
'Well, you can say that if you like,' said the priest.
'Boing, Boing, Boing,' said the Kerryman.

****

A Kerryman was told that if he could answer one general knowledge question he would be given a job as a road sweeper.
'What does Aurora Borealis mean?' asked the interviewer.
'It means I don't get the job,' said the Kerryman.

****

Two Kerrymen went up to Dublin for the All-Ireland Football Final and went out drinking on Friday night. When they woke up on Saturday afternoon, they thought it was Sunday, so they hired a taxi to take them to the big match. The taxi-driver drove them to Landsdowne Road where a big rugby match was in progress. After a while one Kerryman said, 'It's a very rough match isn't it?'
'Yes,' said the other, 'and it must have been a heck of a minor match too. Look at the shape of the ball after it.'

****

What do you see written on the front of a Kerry Mystery Tour bus?
DESTINATION CORK.

****

Have you heard about the Kerry Jew?
He translated the Bible into Hebrew.

****

After the success of the TV blockbuster *Roots,* there is talk of a follow-up set in Kerry. It will be entitled *Boots* and the principal characters will be called *Amandingle* and *Contha Ciaree.*

****

Have you heard about the Kerryman who walked into a record store and asked for the latest single by Marcel Marceau?

****

Kerryman giving directions to a tourist:-
'Drive down the road about two miles until you come to a small whitewashed cottage. Ignore that completely. Then proceed for another bit and turn left where the old milestone used to be. Stick to the tar and you can't miss it.'

****

Kerry circus employees were dissatisfied with their working conditions so they formed a union.
Their first industrial action was a go-slow on the Wall of Death.

****

It is now thought that the word 'bungalow' was invented by two Kerry builders. They were building a two storey house when they ran out of building blocks. 'I'll tell you what,' said one to the other, 'we'll bung a low roof on it and leave it at that.'

****

An old Kerrywoman was explaining to her neighbour that she didn't like teabags.
'By the time you'd have the corners cut off them and the tea taken out of them you'd have been as well off buying a full half pound of tea in a packet in the first place.'

****

An American tourist was being shown around Kerry by a local guide.
'Say Mac,' said the American, 'what's that mountain over there?'
'That's Carrantouhill,' said the Kerryman, 'it's the highest mountain in the world.'
'But what about Mount Everest?' said the American.
'Oh exceptin' those in foreign parts,' said the Kerry-man.

****

Two Kerrymen were sent to jail in a high security prison but they developed an ingenious method of communicating with each other by means of a secret code and banging on the pipes.
However, their scheme broke down when they were transferred to different cells.

****

Kerry Naughts and Crosses 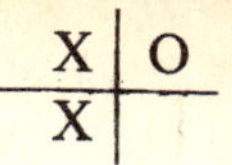

****

Kerry Solitaire Naughts and Crosses.

O	O	O
O	O	O
O	O	O

This game was a draw.

****

Have you heard about the Kerryman who won the Tour de France?
He set off on a lap of honour and hasn't been seen for a month.

****

Then there was the Kerryman who saw a sign:-

KEEP DEATH OFF THE ROADS

so he drove his car up on the footpath.

****

A Kerryman was asked if he would buy a nuclear fall-out shelter in case of a nuclear attack.
'They're a bit expensive,' he replied, 'I think I'll wait and see if I can pick up a good cheap second-hand one.'

****

Customer in Kerry Restaurant: 'I'll have asparagus.'
Kerry Waiter: 'We don't serve sparrows, but how did you know my name was Gus?'

****

The Annual General Meeting of the Kerry Claustrophobia Society has just been held.
Only one member turned up at the hall and he kept shouting, 'let me out, let me out.'

****

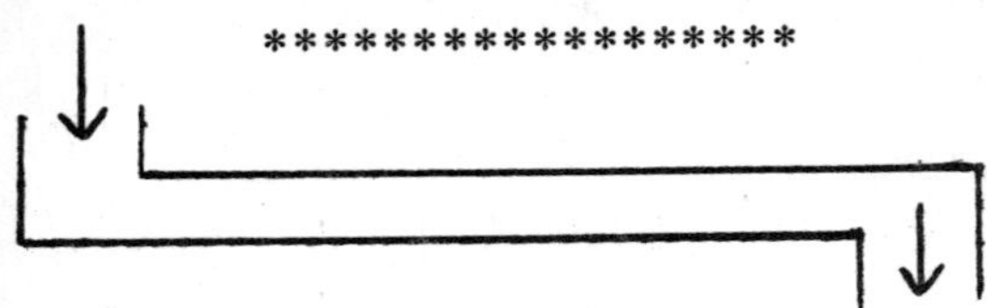

The Famous Kerry Maze – a rescue service is available for those who get lost inside. Some Kerrymen have difficulty finding their way in.

****

Sign in a Kerry shop:

NO DISSATISFIED CUSTOMER IS EVER ALLOWED TO LEAVE THE SHOP.

****

A tourist in a little Kerry village noticed that the two clocks on the church tower showed different times, so he asked a Kerryman to explain.
'Look,' said the Kerryman, 'if both clocks showed the same time, we would need only one clock.'

****

Have you heard about the Kerry footballer who scored a goal in the All-Ireland Final?
He missed it on the action replay.

****

A Kerryman took a body-building course from Charles Atlas. After it was over, he wrote the following letter:

Dear Sir,

I have now finished the course, so please send on the muscles.

****

A Kerryman was in court charged with stealing a cow.
'How do you plead?' asked the judge.
'Not guilty,' answered the Kerryman.
'Is this the first time you've been up before me?' asked the judge.
'I don't know,' said the Kerryman, 'what time do you get up at?'
'No,' said the judge, 'I mean is this the first time you've been in court?'
'Yes,' said the Kerryman, 'I've never stolen anything before.'
The court erupted with laughter so the judge shouted 'order, order.'
'I'll have a pint,' said the Kerryman.

****

It was the Kerry chess championships and the two Kerry grandmasters were sitting with their heads bent over the board, contemplating their strategies. Radio, television and the newspapers waited with bated breath for the next move. Hours went by and there was no sign of anything happening. Then one of the Kerry grandmasters looked up and said, 'Oh! is it my move?'

****

Notice in a Kerry pub:

THE MANAGEMENT WILL NOT BE RESPONSIBLE FOR ANY INJURIES INCURRED IN THE MAD RUSH FOR THE DOOR AT CLOSING TIME.

****

A French lady settled in Kerry so the local coal merchant decided to call on her to see if she required any coal.
'How do you deliver your coal?' she asked him.
'You have a choice,' said the Kerryman, 'you can have it coal de sack or a la cart.'

****

A Kerryman and his wife were going on a picnic so they drove out into the countryside, parked their car and walked a few miles in the woods.
'I hope you've remembered to put the car keys in a safe place,' said the Kerrywoman.
'Of course,' said the Kerryman, 'I've locked them in the boot.'

****

A tourist travelling in Kerry saw a very dangerous unprotected cliff with no warning notice on it, so he asked a Kerryman why this was the case.
'Well,' said the Kerryman, 'we did have a warning notice, but nobody ever fell over the cliff, so we took the notice away.'

****

A Kerry economist has just come up with a fantastic new plan to shorten the dole queue.
He suggests that the unemployed should be lined up four abreast.

****

'Can you play the violin?' a Kerryman was asked in an interview.
'I don't know,' he replied, 'I've never tried'.

****

'A thermos flask is a wonderful invention,' said a Kerryman, 'but there's one thing about it I cannot understand. If you put hot tea in the flask, it keeps hot, but if you put chilled orange juice in it, it keeps it cold; how does it know?'

****

A Kerryman was sent to jail and was sharing a cell with two others.
'What are you in for?' he asked the first.
'Stealing a few bales of straw,' he replied.
'And how long did you get?' asked the Kerryman.
'Six months,' he replied.
'And what are you in for?' he asked the second.
'Rape,' he replied.
'And how long did you get?'
'Seven years,' he replied.
'Heavens above,' said the Kerryman, 'you must have stolen a whole acre of it.'

****

First Kerry Businessman: 'How is business?'
Second Kerry Businessman: 'Terrible, it's the worst year I can ever remember. Even the people who never pay me haven't bought anything this year.'

****

A Kerryman was on trial for stealing a motorcar. He explained that the car was parked outside a cemetery and that he had taken it because he thought the owner was dead.

****

A Kerryman was told by his bank manager that his current account was five hundred pounds overdrawn and that he would have to balance it at once.
'I'm terribly sorry about that,' said the Kerryman, 'and I'll see to it immediately. Can I give you a cheque?'

****

Have you heard about the Kerryman who applied for an unlisted telephone number because he didn't have a telephone?

****

A Kerryman's explanation of the yellow lines on the roads:-
One yellow line means you have to park with two wheels on the pavement: Two yellow lines mean you have to park with all four wheels on the pavement.

****

A Kerryman received a demand from the Income Tax people, so he sent them the following reply:-
Dear Sir,
I have read your very interesting prospectus but I wish to inform you that I don't want to join your club.

****

Have you heard about the Kerryman who refused to make a will?
He thought it would be a dead giveaway to his relatives.

****

A Kerry jarvey was driving a tourist around the Lakes of Killarney.
'Look,' said the tourist, 'that's the thinnest horse I've ever seen in my life – why don't you fatten him up a bit?
'Fatten him up, is it?' said the Kerryman, 'the poor beast can hardly carry all the meat that's on him now.'

****

A Kerryman was sentenced to a total of 500 years in prison for a series of crimes he had committed. He appealed and got his sentence reduced to 400 years.

****

Have you heard about the Kerryman who bought a paper shop?
It blew away.

****

A Kerry explorer was heading for the North Pole with his faithful dog Rover. However, he ran out of food and was forced to eat the poor old dog. As he licked the bones clean, he said, 'poor old Rover would have loved those bones.'

****

A Kerrywoman was addressing the Annual General Meeting of the Widows' Association and she told her listeners:-

'I'm very glad to announce a large increase in membership since last year.'

****

Two Kerrymen escaped from jail and were being followed by the police with tracker dogs. The two Kerrymen decided to climb up into the trees in order to escape. As the dogs came sniffing at the base of the tree where the first Kerryman was hiding he went, 'maiow, maiow'.
'Come away,' said the policeman, 'that's only a cat.'
The dogs then began to sniff at the base of the tree where the second Kerryman was hiding.
'Moo, Moo,' went the second Kerryman.

****

Sign in a Kerry Auctioneers:-

THE HIGHEST BIDDER TO BE THE PURCHASER UNLESS SOMEBODY BIDS MORE.

****

During a recent lightning electricity strike a Kerryman was stuck on an escalator in a big store for over two hours.

****

How do you recognise a Kerryman's motor car? Windscreen wipers on the inside.

****

Kerry boxer (during a break in a fight): 'How am I doing, Coach?'

Coach: 'Let me put it his way – you'll have to knock him out now to get a draw.'

****

Have you heard about the Kerry jellyfish?
It set.

****

A Kerryman was one of the world's most famous clairvoyants.
He even knew beforehand the day he would die because the judge told him.

****

The EEC road fund has just given a hundred million pounds to improve the Kerry Bypass.
It's going to be used to repair the Cork-Limerick road.

****

Sign seen in Kerry:–

METRICATION OFFICE: – 100 YARDS.

****

A Kerryman and his wife had a pretty rough marriage – they had four endorsements on their marriage licence.

****

A Kerryman called round to see his doctor.
'How are you?' asked the doctor, 'I haven't seen you for ages.'
'That's right,' said the Kerryman, 'I haven't been very well.'

****

A Kerryman at the theatre was looking for the Gentlemen's Toilet so he asked the doorman where it was.
'Go down the corridor,' said the doorman, 'turn left and the urinal is there on your right.'
'Actually,' said the Kerryman, 'what I really want is the arsenal.'

****

A Kerryman was seen leaving the theatre at the interval during a new play.
'Excuse me sir,' said the doorman, 'isn't the play to your liking?'
'It's not that at all,' said the Kerryman, 'it's just that the programme says that the second act takes place two weeks later and my mother told me to be home before midnight.'

****

A Kerry teenage girl went to her father and asked him if she could have some money to go and see *Grease.*
He bought her a return ticket to Athens.

****

Have you heard about the Kerry typist who thought that punctuation meant being at the office in time every morning?

****

A Kerryman opened an antique shop and one day an American tourist came in and offered him £10 for an antique vase.
'Take it, though it cost me £20 to buy.'
'But how on earth do you manage to stay in business at that rate?' asked the astonished American.
'Sssh,' said the Kerryman, 'I just make a wrong entry in the ledger.'

****

Four Kerrymen were playing poker while a Corkman looked on. At one stage the Corkman spotted the dealer giving himself four aces from the bottom of the deck. When he drew the attention of the other three Kerrymen to what had happened, one of them said casually, 'what of it, wasn't it his deal?'

****

A landlord had a Kerryman staying in one of his flats so to make sure the central heating was maintained at the correct temperature he supplied the Kerryman with a thermometer.
'Do you know how to use it?' he asked him.
'Yes,' said the Kerryman, 'I sit and watch it until it rises over the critical temperature and then I take it into the garden to cool.'

****

Two Kerrymen, one very fat and the other very thin, once decided to fight a duel with pistols. Their seconds decided that the thin man had an unfair advantage because of the bigger target that the fat man presented. Finally they agreed that the figure of the thin man be chalked on the body of the fat man and that any bullets hitting the fat man outside the line would not count.

****

An old Kerryman was due to go into hospital for an operation for many years, so he finally plucked up the courage. As soon as he arrived at the hospital he was given a thorough bath.
'Well,' he said to himself, 'thank goodness that's over, I've been dreading that operation for years.'

****

Have you heard about the Kerry string quartet? It would have been a sextet only two of them were refused bail.

****

A Kerryman was one of the world's top organists but he had to retire.
His monkey died.

****

Have you heard about the Kerry fire extinguisher factory?
It was burned to the ground.

****

A Society lady went to a famous Kerry artist and asked him if he would paint a portrait of her in the nude for £1,000.
'Certainly,' said the Kerryman, 'but can I leave my socks on because I must have somewhere to put my brushes.'

****

Have you heard about the Kerry cow who went out for a night and drank more than was good for her?
She woke up with a terrible hangunder.

****

Newspaper report of a Kerry funeral: 'At the graveside the son-in-law of the deceased collapsed and died. Naturally this threw a gloom over the entire proceedings.'

****

Have you heard about the Kerryman who used to rub linament on his head?
He thought it would make him smart.

****

Here is a sad little story about a Kerryman with two wooden legs. Fire broke out in his house and he was burned to the ground. He tried to claim money from the insurance company, but he was told he didn't have a leg to stand on. In fact he was accused of arson and being a low down bum.

****

Have you heard about the Kerryman who thought that a transistor was a nun who wore mens' clothes?

****

A Kerryman emigrated to America and one of the first sights he saw was a dead millionaire being buried. The millionaire was dressed in a mohair suit and was encased in a golden coffin studded with diamonds.

'Now that,' said the Kerryman, 'is what I call really living.'

****

A newly rich Kerryman stayed the night in a big Dublin hotel. Next morning the porter asked him if had slept well.

'Not really,' said the Kerryman, 'I was afraid that somebody would want to take a bath and the only way to the bathroom was through my bedroom.'

****

Have you heard about the Kerryman who thought that a knighthood was a cap for keeping his ears warm when he was asleep?

****

A doctor was treating a Kerrywoman for her nerves and having given her a complete examination informed her that she had acute paranoia.
'Look doctor,' she told him, 'I've come here to be treated, not to be admired.'

****

NEWSFLASH!!

Thieves escaped with over half a million pounds from a Kerry bank last night.
Police are baffled trying to figure out the motive for the crime.

****

Have you heard about the Kerryman who thought that a discotheque was a Cork traffic warden?

****

A Kerryman claimed he had a talking dog who was a genius at Mathematics. He used to ask him what five minus three minus two was, and the dog used to say nothing.

****

Some Kerry wills:-

(i) I leave all my money and possessions to the doctor that will pull me through my final illness.

(ii) To my eldest son I leave the farm and to my second son I leave my seat in the Dail.

(iii) I leave everything to myself.

****

A Kerryman and his wife were on their honeymoon in a big hotel. About one o'clock the Kerryman's wife awoke and said she was thirsty so he went down the corridor and got her a drink of water. About two o'clock, she awoke again so the Kerryman got her another drink. Finally, she woke at three o'clock and again said she was thirsty, so once again the Kerryman set off down the corridor. About half an hour later he returned with a glass of water.
'What kept you so long?' she asked him.
'Sorry for the delay,' said the Kerryman, 'but there was a fellow sitting on the well.'

****

A Kerry inventor once came up with the idea of a bar of soap with a hole in the centre. He claimed there wouldn't be any of those awkward little pieces of soap left at the end.

****

A Kerryman went into a bar, ordered a bottle of whiskey and proceeded to drink every drop of it. Then, he got up and started to leave.
'Hey,' said the bartender, 'how about paying for the whiskey?'
'Look,' said the Kerryman, 'did you pay for it?'
'Of course I did,' said the barman.
'Well there's no point in both of us paying for it, is there?' said the Kerryman, and walked out.

****

Have you heard about the Kerrywoman who was asked what she would do if her hot pants went on fire?
She said she would put out the blaze with her panty hose.

****

A Kerryman buying a pair of shoes was asked by the sales assistant what size shoes he took.
'I take size eights,' said the Kerryman, 'but I always find they're a bit tight for me, so I think I'll try on a pair of size nines for a start.'

****

'Is this soldier dangerously wounded?' a Kerry doctor was asked.
'Two of the wounds are fatal,' he replied, 'but the third can be cured, provided the patient gets a few weeks rest.'

****

Have you heard about the Kerryman who went surf riding?
His horse got drowned.

****

Two Kerrymen were sitting by the seashore watching the dredger at work in the harbour.
'Let's go home,' said one Kerryman, 'I've seen enough.'
'No,' said the second, 'I'm not going until I've seen the last of those buckets coming up out of the water. There's been over a thousand of them so far so there couldn't be many left.'

****

Tourist in Kerry restaurant: 'I ordered French sardines. Are you sure these sardines you just served me are French?'
Kerry Waiter: 'I couldn't say sir, they were past speaking when we opened the tin.'

****

'There's one thing we must admire the Chinese for,' exclaimed a Kerryman, 'and that's for learning to speak their own language.'

****

Kerry doctor: 'Have you taken that box of pills I prescribed for you?'
Kerry patient: 'I took the whole box, but I don't feel a bit better yet.'
Kerry doctor: 'Just wait until the lid comes off.'

****

'Has anybody ever been lost in this lake?' a tourist once asked a Kerryman boatman.
'No,' said the Kerryman, 'nobody has ever been lost here. My brother was drowned here last month but they found him two days later.'

****

Two very seasick Kerryman were on the boat to England. One said to the other: 'Mick, for God's sake ask the captain to stop the ship for a few minutes until I get a rest, or I'll have to get out and walk.'

****

'I was that strong when I was a child,' boasted a Kerryman, 'that I could lift up my own pram with myself inside it.'

****

One Kerryman was telling another about his travels and adventures in Africa. 'I once saw a man with his hands tied behind his back being beheaded,' he told him, 'and do you know what happened? – he picked up his head and put it back on his shoulders again.'
'How could he do that?' asked the second Kerryman, 'when his hands were tied behind his back?'
'You fool,' said the first Kerryman, 'couldn't he pick it up with his teeth.'

****

A Kerryman received his army conscription papers so he wrote back saying that he couldn't join because he had a wooden leg. A second letter arrived asking him to give further details of how he came to have a wooden leg. He replied as follows:-

My father had a wooden leg and so had his father before him. It runs in the family.

****

Kerry foreman: 'Where did you put that sledge hammer I gave you?'
Kerry workman: 'I can't find it – I must have lost it.'
Kerry foreman: 'I'll break every bone in your body with it if you don't find it.'

****

Two Kerrymen were working on a building site when one of them fell a hundred feet to the ground. The other Kerryman rushed to his side and shouted, 'Mick, are you killed? If you're dead speak to me.' Mick opened one eye and said, 'no, Tim, I'm not dead, I'm merely knocked speechless.'

****

A Kerryman went to confession and told the priest that he had stolen some turf.
'How much turf did you steal?' asked the priest.
'I may as well confess to stealing a full stack, because I'm going back for the rest of it tonight.'

****

Verdicts of Kerry juries:

Not guilty, if he'll promise to emigrate.

We find the prisoner guilty and recommend that he be hanged, and we hope it will be a warning to him.

****

A Kerrywoman boasted that her husband was a great animal lover. She claimed he once put his shirt on a bleedin' horse that was scratched.

****

Have you heard about the Kerryman who was invited to a house warming?
He spent the whole night helping to insulate the attic.

****

A Kerryman and his wife had trouble in planning their family so their local parish priest advised them to use the rhythm method.
'It's all very well for him to talk,' said the Kerryman, 'but where am I going to get a ceili band at one o'clock in the morning?'

****

It was two Kerrymen who kidnapped the body of Charlie Chaplin.
They threatened to shoot him if they weren't paid a million pounds ransom.

****

A Kerryman went to a dance but wasn't having much success with the girls so he asked his friend for advice.
'Whisper something romantic in her ear,' said the friend, 'girls seem to like that sort of thing.'
A few minutes later the Kerryman returned with a black eye.
'What on earth is the matter,' asked the friend, 'did you whisper something romantic in her ear?'
'I did,' said the Kerryman.
'And what did you whisper?' asked the friend.
'Well,' said the Kerryman, 'I whispered the most romantic thing I could think of; I told her she didn't sweat much for such a fat girl.'

****

Have you heard about the Kerryman who thought that a naval destroyer was a hula-hoop with spikes?

****

Have you heard about the Kerry farmer who went away for the weekend and forgot to unhitch one of his cows from the milking machine?
When he returned he found that the cow had been turned inside out.

****

Two Kerrymen went into a cafe to have a cup of tea. They were given a sugar bowl filled with sugar lumps. 'Hold on,' said the first Kerryman, 'I haven't been given a teaspoon.'
'That's all right, I've got two,' said the second Kerryman breaking the sugar tongs.

****

Have you heard about the Kerryman who put his television set in the oven?
He wanted to have a TV dinner.

****

Then there was the Kerryman who had one arm shorter than the other.
He got a job as a shorthand typist.

****

A Kerryman was asked if he would join a nudist colony. He refused, saying that if Nature had intended him to be a nudist, he would have been born without any clothes on.

****

A big game hunter was showing a Kerryman the heads of all the animals he had shot, mounted on his living-room wall.
'If we go into the other room,' asked the Kerryman, 'can we see the other end of the animals?'

****

Have you heard about the Kerryman who thought that a metronome was a dwarf who lived in the Paris underground?

****

Have you heard about the Kerryman who was hoping to get a no claims bonus on his life insurance?

****

First Kerryman: 'My uncle died during a tightrope performance.'
Second Kerryman: 'I didn't know he worked in a circus.'
First Kerryman: 'He didn't – he was hanged.'

****

A Kerryman was being interviewed for a life insurance policy.
'Have you ever had an accident?' asked the clerk.
'No,' said the Kerryman, 'but once I was kicked by a horse and trampled on.'
'Don't you consider those accidents?' asked the clerk.
'No,' said the Kerryman, 'he did it on purpose.'

****

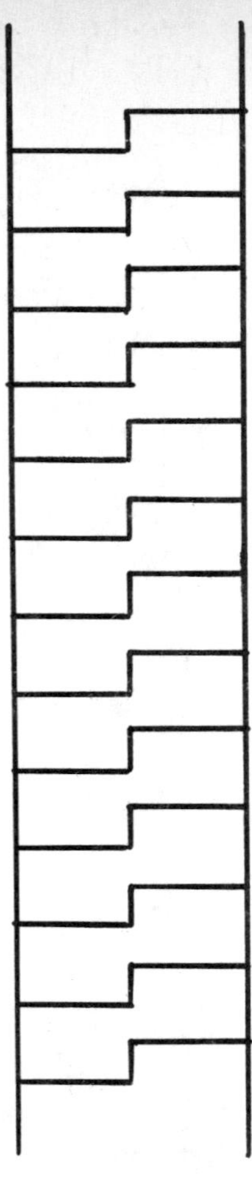

Ladder for a Kerryman with a limp

Have you heard about the Kerry atheist?
He used to say 'I'm an atheist, thank God.'

****

Have you heard about the Kerry lifeguard?
He was trying to give a fellow he had rescued artificial respiration, but the fellow kept getting up and walking away.

****

Have you heard about the Kerry streaker?
He forgot to take his clothes off.

****

A Kerry worm was crawling up out of the ground when he saw the most beautiful worm he had ever seen crawling up out of the ground near him.
'Say baby,' he said, 'how about you and me getting together?'
'We already are,' came the reply, 'I'm your other end.'

****

Have you heard about the Kerry ghost?
He didn't believe in people.

****

What does a Kerryman use for a pocket calculator?
A rabbit – because he heard that rabbits multiply rapidly.

****

Have you heard about the Kerryman who ate twenty packets of cornflakes?
He died of sunstroke.

****

A tourist holidaying in Kerry was astonished to find a pub open and filled with drinkers at two o'clock in the morning.
'Say,' he said to the barman, 'when do the pubs shut around here?'
'About the middle of October,' said the barman.

****

A tourist was being driven around Kerry by a local jarvey when he saw a fine house up on a hill.
'Who lives there?' he asked.
'The late widow O'Keeffe,' said the jarvey.
'When did she die?' asked the tourist.
'If she had lived until next Tuesday,' said the jarvey, 'she would have been dead a year.'

****

Have you heard about the Kerryman who went to a Freemason and asked him if he would build him a house for nothing?

****

Have you heard about the Kerryman who went on a sea voyage and complained because he wasn't invited to dine at the Captain's table?
He was told that dining at the Captain's table wasn't the usual custom on the Killimer car ferry.

****

Have you heard about the Kerry mosquito?
He caught malaria.

****

A Kerryman was applying for a credit card and the manager of the Credit Card Company asked him if he had much money in the bank.
'I have,' said the Kerryman.
'How much?' asked the manager.
'I don't know exactly,' said the Kerryman, 'I haven't shaken it lately.'

****

Have you heard about the Kerry glass blower who inhaled instead of exhaling?
He got a pane in the stomach.

****

Have you heard about the Kerryman who won a trip to Japan in a raffle?
He's still out there trying to win a trip back.

****

A Kerryman went into a big store and asked if he could buy a thermometer.
'Certainly sir,' said the clerk, 'would you like a Centigrade or a Fahrenheit one?'
'Which is the better brand?' asked the Kerryman.

****

A Kerryman travelling by train told the ticket inspector that he wanted to get off at a certain village.
'I'm afraid we don't stop here sir,' said the inspector.
'Could you stop long enough for me to let my wife know that I'm being carried through?' asked the Kerryman.

****

Have you heard about the Kerry version of Gemini Man?
He presses a button and his watch disappears.

****

A Kerryman called at his garage and asked if he could buy a new dip-stick for his car.
'What's the matter with the old one?' asked the attendant.
'It's too short,' said the Kerryman, 'It won't reach down to the oil.'

****

Have you heard about the Kerryman who joined the Mafia and started a protection racket?
He threatened to beat people up if they paid him money.

****

A Kerryman went into an old fashioned grocery store with a big jar and asked the grocer to fill it up with treacle.
The grocer did so and said, 'There you are sir, now where is your money?'
'I left it at the bottom of the jar,' said the Kerryman.

****

A Kerryman has just set up a valuable new service for citizens of Cork city.
He does invisible mending on parking discs at twenty pence each.

****

A Kerryman working in an office was given custody of the only key of the mailbox. However, he went on holidays and took the key with him, so the manager phoned him up and told him the position.
The Kerryman then returned the key immediately by post.

****

A Kerryman visited Paris and when he returned home he was asked what he thought of the Eiffel Tower. 'It's all very nice,' he replied, 'but they'll never get it off the ground.'

****

A Kerryman joined the police force and after a few months he was summoned before the district inspector. 'I'm putting you on night patrol next week,' said the inspector, 'I hope you're prepared for it.'
'Certainly,' said the Kerryman, 'my mother is going to come with me until I get used to it.'

****

Two Kerrymen were on holiday in Majorca, stretched out on the beach soaking in the sun.
'Hey,' said one to the other, 'isn't to-day the day they're playing the county football final back home in Kerry.'
'Yes,' said the other Kerryman, 'and they have a nice day for it too.'

****

Have you heard about the Kerryman who gave up voting in general elections? He said no matter who he voted for the government always won.

****

A Kerryman was hitch hiking when he was picked up by a fellow driving a Mercedes.
'What's that on the front of the car?' asked the Kerryman, pointing to the three pronged Mercedes emblem surrounded by a circle.
'That's the sights of my front gun,' said the fellow who was a bit of a joker, 'I use it to shoot cyclists.'
'There's one in front of us now,' said the Kerryman. 'Show me how it works.'
As they passed by, the driver made some convincing shot-like noises and said 'I'm afraid we missed him.'
'No we didn't,' said the Kerryman, 'I got him with the door of the car as we went by.'

****

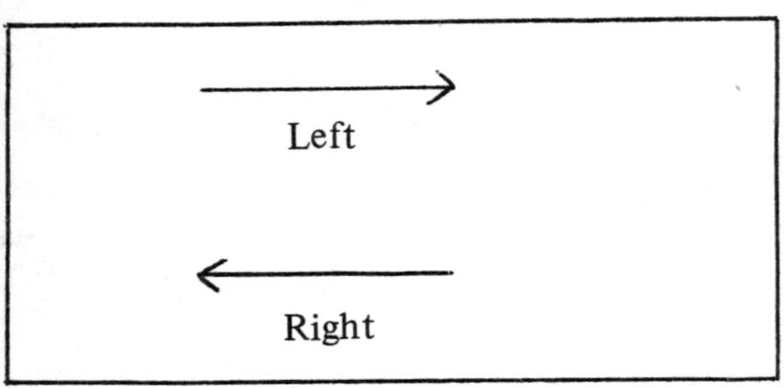

Kerry Army Manual

****

A Kerryman opposed the abolition of capital punishment because if it were abolished it would be unfair to all those who had been executed over the years.

****

The Irish skating championships were reaching a climax when the final competitor had a bit of a mishap. He slipped just as he was entering the rink, slid across the floor on his rear end, and demolished the judges' table with his feet.

'Could I have your marks please, just for the record,' said the chief official.

'0.0,' said the Dublin judge;

'0.0,' said the Galway judge;

'0.0,' said the Cork judge;

'9.9,' said the Kerry judge;

'Hold on a moment,' said the chief official to the Kerry judge, 'how can you award such a high score for such a terrible performance?'

'Well,' said the Kerry judge, 'you've got to make allowances – it's as slippery as hell out there.'

****

Two Kerrymen were out hunting when one of them saw a rabbit.

'Quick,' said the first Kerryman, 'shoot it.'

'I can't', said the second, 'my gun isn't loaded.'

'Well,' said the first Kerryman, 'you know that, and I know that, but the rabbit doesn't know.'

****

Have you heard about the Kerry inventor?

He's just come up with a brand new idea – ejector seats for helicopters.

****

What do the numbers 1798 and 1916 have in common?
Adjoining rooms in a Kerry hotel.

****

Have you heard about the Kerry rabbit who got caught in a trap by his leg?
He chewed off three of his legs and he was still caught in the trap.

****

A Kerryman applied for a job as a bus driver and was given a general knowledge test.
'How far is it from the Earth to the Moon?' he was asked.
'Look,' said the Kerryman, 'if that's going to be my route, I don't want the job.'

****

Have you heard about the Kerry typist?
Every time the little bell on her typewriter rang she thought it was time for a tea break.

****

How do you recognise a submarine designed by a Kerryman?
It's got half doors.

****

How do you make a Kerry cocktail?
Take a half glass of whiskey and add it to another half glass of whiskey.

****

Where is cleanliness next to Godliness?
In a Kerry dictionary.

****

A Kerryman and his wife were staying in a hotel overnight. In the morning she asked him if he had heard all the thunder during the night.
'No,' said the Kerryman, 'I didn't hear a thing; tell me, was it loud?'
'It was the loudest I ever heard,' said the Kerrywoman, 'I thought the hotel would fall over our heads.'
'Why didn't you wake me up?' said the Kerryman, 'you know I can't sleep when there's thunder.'

****

Oil was discovered off the coast of Kerry but during operations one of the oil wells caught fire and went out of control. So they sent for Red Adair, the fire fighter, who flew in by private jet and soon blew the fire out
Afterwards a Kerryman said to him, 'That was terrific, tell me, do you see anything of Ginger Rodgers at all these days?'

****

A Kerryman went into a post office and asked if there were any letters for him.
'I'll see sir,' said the clerk, 'what is your name?'
'You're having me on now because I'm a Kerryman,' said the Kerryman, 'won't you see the name on the envelope.'

****

A Kerryman's wife was about to have a baby so he rang the maternity hospital.
'Don't panic,' said the nurse over the phone, 'we will look after everything. Tell me is this her first baby?'
'No,' said the Kerryman,'this is her husband.'

****

On a summer's day a Kerryman dressed in two heavy overcoats was perspiring heavily as he painted his house.
'Why are you dressed like that?' asked a friend.
'The instructions on the can,' said the Kerryman, 'said to put on at least two coats.'

****

Have you heard about the Kerryman who thought that bualadh bos meant a collision between two C.I.E. doubledeckers?

****

Have you heard about the Kerryman who entered in a slow bicycle race?
He came first.

****

Have you heard about the little Kerry seaside village where the action was a little on the slow side?
The tide went out one day and never came back in again.

****

A Kerryman went ice skating on a frozen lake but was warned that the ice was very thin.
'Not to worry,' he said 'I'll skate on one foot.'

****

A fellow hired a Kerryman as his gardener and asked him how to tell young seedlings from weeds.
'Well,' said the Kerryman, 'the only sure way is to pull them all out and if they come up again they're weeds.'

****

A Kerryman carrying a newspaper walked into a pub and asked the barman if he could tell him what date it was.
'I'm not quite sure,' said the barman, 'but why don't you look at you newspaper?'.
'It's no good,' said the Kerryman, 'it's yesterday's.'

****

Policeman: 'Come out of that river, there's no bathing allowed in there.'
Kerryman: 'The laugh's on you, I'm not bathing, I'm drowning.'

****

Circus Owner: 'You left the door of the lion's cage open all night last night.'
Kerryman: 'What matter, sure nobody in his senses would bother stealing a lion.'

****

Lecturer: 'Here is a list of statistics about Kerry farmers broken down by age and sex.'
Voice from the back: 'What about the drink?'

****

Have you heard about the Kerryman who went into the G.P.O. and asked the girl behind the counter if he could buy a stamped addressed envelope?

****

A Kerryman was living in digs with a number of practical jokers. One night, when he was asleep, they shaved off his fine head of hair and left him as bald as an egg. Rushing out to work in the morning, he happened to glance in the mirror.
'Crickey,' said the Kerryman, 'the landlady has called the wrong man.'

****

Have you heard about the Kerryman who did a hundred yards in three seconds wearing his wellingtons? He fell over a cliff.

****

Kerry teacher's definition of an audiovisual aid – 'do you see this stick and do you hear what I'm saying?'

****

Have you heard about the two Kerry astronauts who landed on the moon?
They went on a spacewalk, slammed the door of the spacecraft and locked the key inside.

****

Have you heard about the Kerry scientist who claimed to be cleverer than Einstein?
Well, only four men are supposed to have been able to understand Einstein's Theory of Relativity, but nobody could understand the Kerryman's theory.

****

A Kerryman in a Psychiatrist's waiting room was running around, first bouncing his head off one wall and then off another. Then he tried to put his head into the pocket of a little man sitting in the corner.
'What's the matter with you?' said the little man.
'I'm a billiard ball,' said the Kerryman.
'Good heavens,' said the little man, 'come to the head of the queue immediately.'

****

'How come,' said a Kerry sergeant to his men, 'that you allowed the most wanted man in the country to escape from the building? I told you to surround the building and watch all the exits.'
'We did, but he must have escaped by one of the entrances.'

****

A Kerry lad on the run from the Black and Tans was having a quick cup of tea in the back kitchen of his parents' house, when word came that the soldiers were on his trail. Quick as a flash he bolted out the back door and ran up the mountain side like a hare. The sergeant shouted to the lad's father who was digging in the back garden.
'Stop that man at once and bring him back.'
The Kerryman shouted up the mountain after his son – 'Come back here Danjoe, and let the gentleman shoot you.'

****

A Kerryman used to take six lumps of sugar in his tea. However, he never stirred it because he didn't like it too sweet.

****

How do you recognise a Kerry striptease artiste?
She's got a sugan for a G-string.

****

A Kerryman was taking his driving test and to the examiner's amazement he went straight through a red light.
'Why did you do that?' he asked the Kerryman, 'we might have been killed.'
'Not to worry,' grinned the Kerryman, 'the brother, who's an expert driver, told me to drive through the red – he's been doing it for years and he's never had an accident.'
A couple of minutes later the Kerryman drove straight through another red light.
'Look,' screamed the examiner, 'you really are trying to kill me.'
Then they came to a green light and the Kerryman slammed on his brakes nearly sending the examiner through the windscreen.
'What the heck did you do that for?' he roared.
'I always stop when the lights are green,' explained the Kerryman; 'after all the brother might be coming the other way.'

****

Two Kerrymen played a game of snooker but didn't pot a single ball all night.
'Next time,' said one of them, 'how about taking that wooden triangle from around the balls?'

****

THICKSILVER

When the television quiz show THICKSILVER visited Kerry recently there were some amusing answers to questions. [Kerrymen will smile, remembering the visit of THICKSILVER to Cork.]

****

What's your name?
Stop the lights.

****

What was Hitler's first name?
Would it be Heil?

****

Who were Adam and Eve's children?
That's a trick question – Adam and Eve had no children.

****

In Anatomy, where is the lumbar region?
Is it the north of Canada?

****

How many degrees in a circle?
How big is the circle?

****

What is meant by general amnesty?
Was he in the American army?

****

What is backgammon?
It it a sort of rasher?

****

How would you make a cigarette lighter?
Take out the tobacco.

****

What name is given to a male bee?
Would it be a wasp?

****

What rugby player has been capped most times for Ireland?
Would it be A.N. OTHER?

****

What is the Ayatullah famous for?
Isn't he the fellow that founded the ceili band?

****

Who was the mythical being, half man and half beast?
Was it Buffalo Bill?

****

How do you spell Tipperary?
Do you mean the town or the county?

****

Finally, there was the Kerryman who was a contestant on MASTERMIND. He chose as his special subject 'Polish Popes of the 20th century.'

****

KERRYMAN HIT BACK OFFICIALLY

The following jokes have just been officially released by the Association for the Prevention of Cruelty to Kerrymen.

****

How do you score a goal in an All-Ireland Final?
Call out the goalkeeper.

****

The EEC have just given ten million pounds for the building of three huge new looney bins. One is in Brussels, one is in London, and they're putting a roof over Dublin.

****

A new police inspector was assigned to Kerry, so before the announcement of his appointment was made, he slipped down to Kerry, incognito, to see what the situation was like.
One night, near midnight, he met the local Garda and asked him if he knew any place where he could get a drink after hours.
'Don't worry,' said the Garda, 'I'll look after you,' and he took the shocked new inspector to a pub where they had a whale of a time in the company of dozens of Kerrymen.
At about 4 a.m. the inspector turned to the Garda and said, 'what would your Sergeant say if he could see you now?'
'He'd say wasn't I the cute lad to be drinking with the new inspector,' smiled the Kerry Garda.

****

MORE MERCIER BESTSELLERS

THE BOOK OF KERRYMAN JOKES :
Des MacHale.

JOKES FROM THE PUBS OF IRELAND :
James N. Healy.

THE WORST KERRYMAN JOKES :
Des MacHale.

THE BOOK OF KERRYWOMAN JOKES:
Laura Stack.

THE BOOK OF KERRYMAN RIDDLES :
Sonnie O'Reilly.

ENGLISHMAN JOKES FOR IRISHMEN :
Des MacHale.

THE BOOK OF ELEPHANT JOKES:
Des McHale.

IRISH LOVE AND MARRIAGE JOKES :
Des MacHale.

THE BOOK OF CORKMAN JOKES :
Des MacHale.

OFFICIAL IRISH GRAFFITI :
Sean Kilroy.

GRAFFITI FROM THE 'BOGS' OF IRELAND :
Mike G.

THE BUMPER BOOK OF KERRYMAN JOKES :
Des McHale

BALLADS FROM THE PUBS OF IRELAND :
James N. Healy

GEMS OF IRISH WISDOM : IRISH PROVERBS AND SAYINGS :
Padraic O'Farrell

SUPERSTITIONS OF THE IRISH COUNTRY PEOPLE :
Padraic O'Farrell

THE BOOK OF IRISH CURSES :
Patrick C. Power

IRISH FAIRY STORIES FOR CHILDREN :
Edmund Leamy

IRISH FOLK STORIES FOR CHILDREN :
T. Crofton Croker

IN MY FATHER'S TIME :
Eamon Kelly

LETTERS OF A SUCCESSFUL T.D. :
John B. Keane

LETTERS OF A LOVE-HUNGRY FARMER :
John B. Keane

A HISTORY OF IRISH FAIRIES :
Carolyn White